TIME MANAGEMENT:

Learn the Strategies and Secrets of Successful People to Increase your Productivity and Stop Procrastinating for Entrepreneurs, Managers, Workers, Students, Olympic Athletes

Table of Contents

Introduction	5
Chapter 1: Lay the Groundwork for an Effective Routine	7
Building a Great Daily Routine	8
Use Triggers to Spark Creativity	9
Manage Your To-Do List	10
Record Your Commitments	11
Establish a Hard Set Start Time and End Time	12
Chapter 2: The Power of Frequency	**16**
Make Starting Easier	17
Keep Ideas Fresh	18
Keep the Pressure Off	20
Spark Creativity	21
Foster Productivity	23
A Realistic Approach	24
Chapter 3: Making Room for Solitude	**26**
Self-Knowledge	27
Creativity	28
Clarity	30
Energized	31
Confidence	33
Chapter 4: Banish Multitasking	**35**
OHIO Principle	36
Take the Time to Pause	37
Learn How to Say No	39
Choose Your Task	40
Ask Yourself Good Questions	41
Give Permission	42

Chapter 5: Learning to Create Amid Chaos   **44**
   Working at an Optimal Time of the Day   45
   Fences Make Great Neighbors   47
   Discover Real and Virtual Filters   48
   Paying Attention to Your Mental and Physical Health   50

Chapter 6: Using Social Media Mindfully   **53**
   Be Strategic   54
   Engage in Positive Posting   56
   Experience Now, Share Later   57
   Block Out Usage Times   59

Chapter 7: Reconsider Being Constantly Connected   **62**
Chapter 8: Reclaim Self-Respect   **71**
Chapter 9: Letting Go of Perfectionism   **80**
Chapter 10: A Call to Action   **90**
Conclusion   **100**

Introduction

Congratulations on purchasing this book and welcome to *Time Management*. If you are an entrepreneur, manager, worker, student or olympic athlete who is looking to change your approach to your daily routine and get a new perspective to time management, you have come to the right place. *Time Management* will be your guide to getting your life back when it comes to your work-life balance as well as feeling less overwhelmed with your responsibilities and workload. If you find yourself working more than 8 hours a day but not actually accomplishing anything and looking for a change, you have picked up the right book to help you get started.

Time Management will be a workbook to help you change your work behaviors, so you can plan out your days causing less stress and anxiety, while also allowing yourself to accomplish your tasks without wasting your time and getting more work done in the same amount of time. Time management is something that most adults struggle with, and it is an important part of being able to live a successful and fulfilling life that is stress-free. This book will show you how easy it is to manage your time and accomplish all the things you set out to do with your life. We will start out by discussing laying out an effective routine, how powerful frequency is, making room for solitude, and how to reduce the drive to multitask. We will then discuss creating among the chaos, reducing social media usage, and reconsidering being constantly connected to the outside world. Rediscover yourself respect by letting go of perfectionism and finally bring yourself to a call for action and work on your time management today. Once you complete this book, you will be a much better place to manage your time efficiently and effectively going forward.

There are plenty of books on this subject on the market, so thanks again for choosing this one! Every effort was made to ensure it is full of as much useful information as possible. Please enjoy and learn a lot from it!

What you will find in this guide are the strategies that successful people use when they have goals to achieve.

Chapter 1: Lay the Groundwork for an Effective Routine

If you find yourself stuck in a rut with the daily in and out of the work that you are required to do for your job, without much room for anything else or the ability to use your creative mind, you may find that you are not managing your time well. Most people who are engaging in tasks that do not satisfy the creative part of their mind find that they are often bored and wish that they had more time to do the things that they enjoy, rather than spending their lives working. Everyone has bills to pay, and obligations to work and family that they have to satisfy. There is also likely a grey area between the things that we have to do and the things that we want to do in our lives. If you are not careful with how you are spending your time, you are likely going to fill up this grey area with emails and meetings and fulfilling the requests of others, in turn, not leaving room for the type of work you consider important.

What is your motivation for learning how to manage your time? You picked up this book for a reason, whether it is because you are missing out on the meaningful activities you wish you had time to do or spending more time with your family. Are you seeking an overall sense of balance between work and pleasure? As you are at the beginning of this book, take the time to write down your compelling reason. If there was one thing that you could add to your life and daily routine that would make you happier, what would it be? Think about that one thing and write it down and keep it close. We can guarantee that if you read at least a third of the strategies in this book, you will be able to add the activity you are yearning for into your life. This statement you are writing down will provide you a starting point for your journey to becoming someone who can manage their time better, and you will also be able to stay motivated. Although we are aware that it can be a struggle to change your behaviors that are ingrained from daily life, but you will find that it is a lot easier to succeed when you focus on all the things you have to gain from managing your time.

Building a Great Daily Routine

How is it possible to be constantly buckled down doing work while ignoring requests from everyone? You should begin with the common rhythm of your levels of energy. You may have come to notice that there are certain times of the day that allow for focused creativity. This is talked about in society usually as being a "morning person" or an "evening person". This is because of your circadian rhythms for your arousal and mental alertness. You can start to manage your time by figuring out when these high levels of mental energy are for you and then use this time during the day to dedicate to those valuable works that are important to you. If you can help it, you should never book a meeting during this time. You should also not waste any of this time on administrative work. If you allow yourself to focus on the work that you enjoy or want to do more of during your peak energy times, you give yourself the opportunity to focus directly on the task at hand, and you can get more completed with little to no interruption. If you are currently trying to get this work done during your low times, this is likely why you are finding yourself not getting anything done and not being able to stay focused. A shift in your schedule can make all the difference when you pay attention to your natural body rhythm and the times that are of high energy for you and your body.

Use Triggers to Spark Creativity

By use of the word *triggers*, we are referring to a type of symbolic routine that will train your mind to know that it is time to hunker down and get serious about work when all of these things align. If you stick to the same tools, surroundings, and music, for instance, they will slowly become associative triggers for you to enter into your focused zone. Stephen King has a similar routine for when he sits down to begin writing his latest novel. He will begin by getting a glass of water or a cup of tea, depending on the mood he is in that day. He will then sit down for work at a certain time during the day, usually between the half hour of 8 and 8:30 in the morning. He will take a vitamin, turn on his music, sit in the same seat he always sits in and has his papers always arranged in the same position day after day. He believes the cumulative purpose of doing this is so that these things are the same way every single day, and it is a way to tell his mind, *you are going to get to work soon*! Many people who have read or written about time management believe in the systems of having a routine. The mind is easy to teach and knows how to adjust to certain patterns, so training your brain to know when it is time to focus on a specific task is one of the best things you can do to learn how to manage your time better. Once you have established triggers that work for you, you can move on to other steps in the process.

Manage Your To-Do List

It is best for your brain to feel like you are in control of your time if you keep your daily to-do list to a minimum. Follow the practice of filling out your daily to-do list on a 3x3 sticky note and keep it to that amount of space. If it does not fit on the sticky note, it can wait until tomorrow. If you can't fit it on that paper size, how can you expect yourself to get everything done on the same day? If you continue to add to your to-do list during the day, you will likely never finish it by the time you have to leave for the day, and this can make your motivation and drive plummet. Usually, you can find things on your to-do list that can wait until tomorrow. If this is the case, make it wait until tomorrow. The less stress you feel about a never-ending to-do list, the more accomplished you will feel when you leave work for the day, and you have a completed to-do list. Keeping your to-do lists to a minimum will also help you to be less overwhelmed about all of the tasks you have to accomplish. You are likely a very person in your position, and feeling overwhelmed usually has people feeling a motivation block, and they actually end up accomplishing less than they would have if they just limited what they thought they needed to get done that day. Prioritizing your tasks also helps in creating your to-do list because you will obviously need to finish things that have an impending due date over less important administrative tasks that can possibly wait until the end of the week when your schedule can typically slow down.

Record Your Commitments

The next thing you can do to help manage your time is to train yourself to begin recording every commitment you make to yourself and to others in regard to getting work done or meetings and appointments. People who write things down have less of a tendency to forget about it. This means that you are less likely to forget about a project or task you have committed to at work, and you can accomplish it in a reasonable amount of time as opposed to forgetting and having to rush at the last minute to complete it and it not be your best work. Having this as a part of your daily habits will also help you respond to your commitments more quickly as they are likely to become a part of your daily to-do list. You can prioritize your commitments, and those that are more important can get your attention first and get completed with accuracy and co-workers will be much happier working with you on future collaborations. This will ultimately give you peace of mind, and when you are gaining more confidence that you are capturing your responsibilities reliably, you can focus on the tasks you have on hand for that day rather than getting distracted with thoughts of things you could potentially be forgetting. Writing things down and keeping clean and concise lists help you manage your time better because you have everything out in front of you visibly and in a readily available way as opposed to relying on your memory to record everything you need to get done. This is a huge stress reliever for those of us who feel like we do not have enough time in the day to get everything done on the list.

Establish a Hard Set Start Time and End Time

It is important that you set a start time and end time to your workday every day even if you are working alone as a freelancer or if you have a job that allows you to work from home. Once you have established a workday, dedicate different times within that workday to do different activities: creative work, meetings, emails and texts, and IMs, administrative work, and everything else that your job might require you to do. Keeping a set work schedule as you would if you had an office job, or even if you have an office job but not a set amount of hours you are required to work a day, will help keep your tasks to a timetable and will not let it run over into the time that you should be working on other things. You might not complete the task within the allotted amount of time, but this will keep you from working on a task all day, still not getting it done and not accomplishing anything else either. This way, if you do not complete this task, but you have allotted time for 4 other tasks, you will feel more accomplished if you can complete 3 of those tasks as opposed to not accomplishing anything all day. This set schedule can help you avoid workaholism in which you get up super early in the morning and do not go to bed until late at night because you have a set schedule and you end up working all day. This, in theory, sounds like something that all corporations and bosses want, but it is ultimately less productive than it looks. You are less likely to get more done in an open work schedule than a hard edge schedule because you will probably end up getting more distracted without a set routine. Overworking yourself will also lead you to burn out a lot faster than if you get yourself into a hard set schedule and use your time accordingly.

These are just a few tips for things you can do to begin working on your ability to manage your time better. The above suggestions are simply things that you can start to incorporate into your life and daily routines in which you feel like you are at a loss in getting everything done in the time that you have during the day. Setting schedules for yourself and blocking out periods of time to do different things based on your energy levels will help you become your most productive self. Small changes in your current routine will make all the difference when you are trying to become more productive and accomplish everything you have set out to do. Time management will also allow you to work on things that are of interest to you outside of your responsibilities because you will be more likely to get those responsibilities done in less time than it took you before. If you go through your workday where you are just waiting to be in the mood to get something done, you will likely never get there. Setting your intentions and focus on the task at hand while getting your brain into the right mindset to focus on that task will make all the difference. You will be able to cross off more on your to-do list and leave your work at the end of the day feeling more accomplished than you ever have before. This, in turn, can help with your work-life balance, and you will ultimately feel less stressed and constricted by your commitments.

A routine that is truly effective is always going to be unique from person to person. This will be more in fit with your own talent and inclinations. You can take the time to experiment with the building blocks we have provided for you, and you will be able to notice which combination of building blocks and suggestions work for you and what gives you the best foundation for you to feel like you can do your best work effectively. Are you wondering when you will figure out if the new steps you have taken are successful? You will like it is effective when you realize that your daily schedule feels a lot less a routine and more like a ritual you get to partake in daily that allows for not only accomplishing your commitments but also allowing your creativity to flourish. Feel good in knowing that you are well on your way to figuring it all out, and you are not the only one out there who is seeking help and getting advice in where to start. Everyone struggles with managing their time every now and then, but getting yourself on the right path and into a safe and effective routine is the best thing you can do for your creative mind and for your body not to feel burnt out at every turn and at the end of each project and the beginning of another. You will get control back of your schedule, and this book will help you get there with time.

Chapter 2: The Power of Frequency

Although it may seem counterintuitive, there is a lot of power in frequently working on projects and tasks even if it those that you do not enjoy doing. There is a lot of controversy about working every day, but some people actually find that doing a little bit of work every day instead of trying to work for a full block of 8+ hours on some days actually helps them to be more productive and less anxious in the time that they spend working as opposed to working a more traditional day. Even if you are only working short stints of time, say 15 to 20 minutes, you will still find that this kind of frequent work makes it possible to accomplish more, and you will also see that your work is providing a lot more originality than it would have previously pushed yourself through long periods of working hours. If you are frequently working through projects, you will find that you will also accomplish more of the projects on time than you would with the constant distractions of trying to work through long hours. You will likely also produce better work because you are not strained during the times that you are working, and you are putting yourself in a better mindset as well as better working conditions that are more peaceful rather than stressful.

Make Starting Easier

The biggest challenge to any project is getting started. It is always difficult to start something new from scratch, and it gets increasingly harder to enter back into a project after breaks or prolonged time off between working sessions. You are probably experiencing a lack of momentum currently as you are taking long breaks from your work during weekends or when you are trying to cram more work hours into the daylight so you can take extended breaks in your evenings. If you change your routine from working long hours some days and having days off to working consistency every day, you will find that it is easier for you to jump back into projects more quickly and also keep your momentum going. You will never be detached from your work long enough to experience gaps in creativity and work progress. You will also never have to spend time reminding yourself where in your work you finished previously and where you need to pick back up. You will also reduce the amount of time you have to go back and review your work because you are much more likely to remember where you were at before and also be confident in the work you previously created the day before. You will then be able to always keep your work fresh in your mind so even when you are not sitting down working, you will be able to come up with new and exciting ideas that could be of benefit to your work rather than feeling uncreative and not being able to do the type of cognitive problem-solving you are hoping to do to keep your work moving forward. If you keep your projects fresh in your mind, you are much more likely to be able to pick up where you left off with little to no interruption in your flow of creative thinking and problem-solving processes. If you find that it is hardest for you to keep yourself going when you are starting and stopping projects, this is a great tool to implement into your work routine so you can see a reduction in the amount of idle time you are taking to review work and thus wasting creative working time that you could be using to produce more value-added work to the project you are currently in. Working every day may seem like a sure fire way of reaching burn out, but you will find it will actually save you from feeling like you are burnt out rather than working a typical work week.

Keep Ideas Fresh

You will eventually find you are much more likely to see new relationships and fresh connections between your work and new ideas if you are keeping your mind on your projects constantly and you are always thinking about uses related to your work. If you are deep in a project and you keep your mind focused on it, you will find that you can make more connections related to it and you might find it thrilling to discover potential problem-solving solutions you may not have otherwise has the mental space to think up. You will also be able to come up with multiple solutions that you can put into action and recover from sooner if they do not work out as you have hoped for. Being able to keep a running list of ideas rather than holding onto one or two keeps a loss from being much more substantial because you always have a few more to fall back on in times of needing to solve a problem immediately. You might also develop a much more interesting outlook on the world and find it more complex than you previously felt. You might be working the type of job that requires you to have an abundance of material ready and available to put into use, and this will allow you to become more hyperaware of the times and the ideas that have the potential to pull through and keeping a mental folder when the idea flow in. If you are working sporadically, it will make it hard for you to keep your focus both while you are in a work block time and while you are not working but actively working on new ideas. You will find it easier to get blocked, confused, and much more likely to get distracted, and you might even forget what you are trying to finish and aiming to accomplish. When you are working to be a better member of your workgroup, it is much better to keep ideas fresh in your mind because you personally will feel like you are contributing more to your work conversations, and your co-workers and managers will also know that they can rely on you for quality content and they may even look to you for promotion opportunities and give you bigger projects sooner than your peers because of this.

Keep the Pressure Off

If you are currently working on an open topic or problem a week, you can expect the work you are turning out to be good; but you may start to worry about the level of quality of work you are putting out. Sometimes, you may find yourself barely able to bring yourself to do your work. When you can find the mental space to get yourself in front of the computer to work, there may be a feeling of enormous pressure to be brilliant and creative. This may then cause you to be uneasy about your own work and review it with a highly critical eye. You are not accomplishing much work, so what you accomplish has to be what you consider to be above and beyond and extraordinarily good. When you are working every day, you will find that work from one day is not any more important than the work you get done from another. You will always have good work days and bad work days. You will find that some days you may not accomplish much at all, and this is fine because you are working much more steadily. With this lack of anxiety that you are putting on yourself to be a top performer, you are in a better frame of mind to be more playful, and you allow yourself to experiment more in your work and eventually take some positive risks. If something you try to do doesn't work out, you can always adjust your thinking and procedure and try a different approach. You can keep working at this until you find what works the best for you. Even though something work for one person does not mean that it also works for you. Keeping the pressure off yourself opens your mind to focusing more on the creative rather than critiquing your own work, and you will open yourself to being more flexible with yourself and your environment and find that you are producing more quality work without added pressure. Even if you have a day where you do not accomplish much, it is still better than putting out work that is not to the best of your ability. Quality work over assumed pressure will keep you from burning out in your work, and you will feel the benefits of managing your time this way and knowing the work you are putting out is the best you can do.

Spark Creativity

You might be thinking that forcing yourself to work even if you are not in the mood or feeling inspired will make you reduce your standards for your quality of work. What happens is actually the exact opposite. You might be surprised to find out that you can turn out some of your best work when you are continuously grinding out work on a project or task. Creativity can arise from working through a project every day and giving yourself the time to be thinking about it constantly. You will come up with ideas you may not have otherwise even considered because you are creative in your problem-solving rather than taking the same route you always do. Consistently working on something also gets you in the routine of always maintaining a pool of ideas and keeping yourself fertilizing your mind so that you are constantly engaged in all aspects of the project for the entire duration in which it is yours. If you work sporadically, you will then be able to spark creatively sporadically. Thus, if you are constantly working and creating new ideas, you will always be able to spark creativity, especially when you need it the most. You can use this thought process not only in your workflow in trying to manage your time but it can also spread across all areas of your life in which you are feeling that you could be inspired from sparking creativity. For instance, if you are feeling your home is mundane and it seems like the same old routine, you can spark creativity in your home life by creating new weeknight meals or go out for weeknight adventures you may have always been accustomed to keeping for your weekends. If you are always looking for ways to get out of your home routine, you will spark different creative ways to make it more fun and enjoyable for everyone in your family. This will also help you feel closer as you are likely going to be spending more time together in new ways. You can manage your time effectively at work to be home with your family more, and you can also manage your time with your family better by already having new activities to do together and not wasting time trying to figure out what to do. Everyone benefits from living a creative life; it just takes practice, and you will see you can incorporate it in any avenue you want.

Foster Productivity

At this point, it should really come as no surprise that you can get a lot more work done when you are working daily. Keep in mind that the work that is getting completed today will keep the transition into tomorrow's work smooth and pleasant. If you are someone who likes to measure your progress, nothing should be more exciting for you than to be able to see yourself moving closer to the ultimate goal of finishing your project. Each step you are taking will ultimately move you forward in the direction you want to go. This is why daily practices you can incorporate into your routine are so helpful because it keeps you in the environment where you perform your work well and keep you on task. The ultimate goal of being better at time management is to be more productive with the time you use to work, and fostering frequency in your work is a great way to get there. Your continued progress can be inspiring and reassuring, whereas the opposite that you were feeling in panic and despair when you are finding yourself with getting nothing accomplished for a full day's worth of work. A lot of people face fear around procrastination, but it is one thing that a lot of people have trouble getting a handle on and turning it around into productivity. If you can get yourself to procrastinate less by working more frequently, you can quintessentially eliminate it from something to fear in your work life altogether. If you can overcome this fear of procrastination instead of buckling down into it as most people do, you will find that your time is better managed and you are getting more quality work completed that you could have previously thought possible. Productivity is one of the ultimate end goals for time management, and we are all looking to get more accomplished in the time we spend on working so that work does not have to overfull into other aspects of our lives that we have carved out time for and will no longer have time to do if we are not productive. Frequency in our work helps to foster productivity in so many ways, and you can also be on your way to reaping the benefits of it once you can successfully create a space for it within your schedule.

A Realistic Approach

Frequency is helpful when you are working through a project while also juggling obligations from your co-workers and family. Instead of getting yourself in a position of feeling perpetually frustrated with your lack of progress or motivation, or feeling as though you do not have time to work through your project, you can now learn to make the time available for yourself. If you do a little bit every day, you can get a lot more accomplished over the course of months and years than you would have previously. Frequency does not necessarily need to be daily frequency; what is most important is a level of consistency. The more widely part of your work time spreads, the less you will reap the benefits.

Chapter 3: Making Room for Solitude

There will always be people in our lives who need and expect things from us on a daily basis. Our managers and co-workers need us to do our jobs correctly and coordinate on projects within our work environments. Our families need encouragement and acknowledgment and to listen about their days and help with homework. It is only when we are completely alone that we can put down our social masks and truly be ourselves as the most comfortable we are. This is the only time that we can face what we need and how we learn to take care of ourselves while still taking care of our responsibilities and families. We must truly know how to take care of ourselves before we can take care of others successfully. For us to be able to spend the time needed to take care of our responsibilities, we must spend the time we need to recoup from working so hard outside of ourselves. We are not taught growing up how to be in solidarity. We are taught that being alone is lonely. We are accustomed to going from our family homes to school to the workplace and eventually choosing our own families--all of which are positive experiences which we cannot exactly experience solitude. It is easy to associate solitude with painful loneliness, but instead, we strive to fill all of our time with activities and to keep ourselves eternally busy. However, there is a big difference between loneliness and solitude. Solitude is a choice, and it is an empowering feeling. We choose to be alone and disconnect from others to give our minds and body the opportunity to reconnect with ourselves and to figure out what we need to do for us to feel good so that we can continue to succeed in our outside requirements from the world.

Self-Knowledge

When you are alone in solitude, you can solely focus on yourself. This is a great way for you to become more in tune with yourself and your feelings as well as your wants and needs. It gives us a space to observe what is going on within ourselves and for us to find out what is important to us. It is easy to follow the feeling of the crowd when you are in a group of people, but you can truly reflect upon what is important to you as an individual when you are alone. You are also given the opportunity to find out what you truly love and dream about. Self-knowledge is all about finding out who you are as an individual and what your values are as a person. Many people spend their whole lives relying on other people to influence them into the people they believe they should be when in reality, you will not find out who you truly are as a person unless you take the time in solitude to look within yourself and figure it out on your own. If you can focus on yourself during these times of solitude, you will also find that you can increase your levels of awareness when working on your productivity when you are working alone. Getting yourself in the mindset of work every time you are alone will help increase your productivity because you are training your mind when to know it is time to work, and you are less likely to get distracted by the things around you in your environment. Knowing what your distractions are and learning how to avoid them in your workspace is the best way to keep yourself focused through the task at hand, and you will find you are accomplishing a lot more and your productivity is increased. This is especially important to practice if you are a freelancer who is used to working alone in a home office or other type of work setting where you are spending more hours alone than you are with other people. Typically, freelancers are known to get distracted as they are working from home easily, but when you are in a proactive, mindful solitude, you will find that you can curb the distractions and make your work time more productive even if you are at home. Knowing and taking care of yourself first is the best thing that can come from practicing mindful solitude.

Creativity

When you can take the time to calm down the world around you and stop your swirling thoughts about all your responsibilities and commitments, you can change your focus and begin thinking up more creative ideas and endeavors that help you focus on solving problems and using other parts of your brain that you might not be able to work in other types of work environments. We have talked about sparking creativity a lot so far throughout this book, but it is important to understand that if you are not creating things that spark your creativity, you are likely not fulfilled in your work. Creativity is so important in any type of project you are working on even if it is for a typical office environment job. There would be no process improvement ideas if people did not spark creativity in themselves to create a better way of going about a particular task. Allow yourself to be fully immersed in your own thoughts and feelings and you will find that you will be able to spark creative ideas more easily than you would if you are surrounded by a large group of people who are more interested in you completing the tasks they have assigned to you. We should take the time to think through thoughts and issues on our own so that we can form our own opinions and not just follow the opinions of the people we spend the most time with. You will need to form your own ideas so that you are fully confident in the work you produce and that you are fully behind whatever changes you think need to be instituted to solve a problem or finish a project you are working on and are needing to manage your time better to complete it in time and with quality work. Creativity is the backbone for all good projects, and you will find that the more creative you allow yourself to become, the more quality of work you will produce and the better you will get at managing your time because you will always be thinking about the project you are working on. Your mind will always be flowing of creative ideas in which you can use to work on the project or solve whatever problems are weighing on you. Solitude is important to spark that creativity because you will be able to think only your own thoughts and truly know the things that interest you.

Clarity

When you are constantly surrounded by a group of people, you may not be giving yourself the opportunity to slow down and take the time to process a problem or situation in a way that you would if you were able to give yourself some time alone. Solitude gives you the opportunity to take space and prices to process the problems in life, and sometimes, it is difficult to understand emotions. This helps us review and release our emotions, such as anger and frustration, instead of lashing out at our loved ones and coworkers if we are dealing with a lot of workplace stress or we are struggling to complete an important project. Once we can process the emotions in a safe space, we can move past it and begin anew with an open mind and more clarity in finding the solution to the problem that we had previously. If you can take your stress and emotions out of a situation, you are more likely to find logical solutions to problems or projects and you can also implement them right away as opposed to letting your emotions get the best of you and delaying a productive implementation because you are too overwhelmed or stressed out to try to fix a problem or to look for new solutions. Finding clarity within yourself is one of the best ways that you can see from all angles what you need to work on, and it will help you be an all-around better person, as well as an employee and boss. You should always strive to find clarity in your work and yourself so that you can keep your emotions out of the workplace and only come with what you need to get the work done for the day. This will help you stay on task and focused so that you do not find yourself drifting off thinking about other things while you should be completing your work and tasks for the day. Clarity and focus go hand in hand; both are extremely important elements of successful time management. You can have one without the other and be good at managing your time, but if you can strive to have both and implement them into your daily routines, you will find that you can manage your time the most successfully when you have both. Clarity helps in all ways of being a better boss and employee as you are not allowing yourself the opportunity to cloud your mind or judgment with other things that you will not benefit from given the situation you are in.

Energized

If you consider yourself an introvert, you will understand the value of spending time alone for you to get your energy levels back up to a functioning level. A lot of us can see the value in spending time alone because being around a lot of people for hours a day every day can often be exhausting to always be at the top of our game and to be socializing constantly. Spending some time alone in solitude, doing something that you enjoy doing on your own is a great way to bring up your energy and find yourself much more rested and relaxed. Even if you consider yourself an extrovert and find that you get your energy from being around people rather than being alone, it is still a good idea to take the time to rest within yourself so that you can bring your balance back to the center. Being around people may be fun and exciting at the moment, but you should still make a conscious effort to take time and spend quite a time with yourself so you can rest both your body and your mind before beginning to resume spending time with people again. Take a breather and resting for a few hours a day or giving yourself a full day on the weekend, if possible, is a good way to reset your mind and body and will likely help you recover from workplace stress or anxiety that you feel from projects you are currently working on. Taking the time to rest also helps prevent you from getting sick, so you are not trying to work a full-time schedule when you are not feeling at the top of your game both physically and mentally. Feeling rested will also help you feel relaxed within the present moment, you will see the beauty of it, and you can find that inner peace within yourself when you give yourself the opportunity to take a moment to breathe and recuperate from stressful projects and work environments. There is nothing you can do to better yourself than taking a moment to rest to regain your energy before continuing on a task in trying to be more mindful of your time. This can be a hard thing to do for most people who believe that they are more likely to thrive if they keep themselves busy, but if you try to incorporate this into your routine, you will find you are in a much better position to feel like you can manage your time better when you allow yourself that opportunity to take a good rest now and again.

Confidence

Being alone with yourself gives you the opportunity to rely on yourself in ways that you may have found strength in through others. Oftentimes, we rely too heavily on others to build us up and create our confidence when really we should be doing this for ourselves. When you are alone with yourself for an extended period of time, you will find that you have to rely on yourself for these things, and you find the strength and power within yourself to keep your head up and boost your own confidence. When you can do this, you will see that you have more self-confidence, which is important when you are trying to manage your time. If you rely too heavily on others, you will not have the ability to create your own schedule and know what works best for you in your levels of energy, as well as your commitments to accomplishing tasks. You can honor yourself in a way that others cannot, and in turn, you can find that you can create your own schedule and work on your own projects without needing a push from others. This helps with time management because you will know what to work on when, and you will not be sitting idly waiting on others to tell you what you need to do next. You are telling yourself that you are worth it, and you are finding the power within yourself to push yourself through the completion of tasks. Self-confidence is also extremely important for time management because you will not have to rely on anyone to consistently tell you what to do, and you will be more confident in yourself to get things done on your own in your own time but still creating a quality project. Having confidence in yourself does not happen overnight, but developing this while you are working on your time management skill is definitely beneficial to your work life as well as home life because you can rely more on yourself rather than others, and this is an important life skill to have when you are working towards moving up in a company or freelancing projects to begin starting your own company in the future.

Chapter 4: Banish Multitasking

You may be at a point in your life and your career that you are thinking you need to multitask to feel accomplished when your day is over. Research shows that the average person looks at their phone at least 150 times a day. That is an insane amount of time wasted if you think about it! Not only do we have that as a daily habit in our lives but there are also many times where we are likely to find ourselves working on two different tasks or projects at work to try and get all of our assigned work done within the due date or timeframe allotted to complete it. There is much more competition in the corporate world, and many people are feeling the pressure to outperform their coworkers to ensure their spot within the company. This leads to a lot of people working extended hours and taking on multiple projects at a time for them to look like they are on top of it all to their business partners and bosses. Although this seems like a good idea, in theory, this level of multitasking is not only detrimental to your health, but you are likely to be unsuccessful in your ventures while turning in a low-quality level of work because you are trying to do too many things at once. In this chapter, we will take a moment to discuss different techniques you can use to decrease the amount of multitasking you are partaking in to make sure you are using your time effectively. There is nothing worse than working yourself to death with little to no accomplishment on the day in and day out every day you are hard at work at the job. Banishing multitasking will help you regain control of your schedule and learn how to manage your time more effectively.

OHIO Principle

The first thing you can work on to banish your multitasking is actually pretty simple. Instead of switching back and forth between multiple projects throughout the day, use this OHIO principle, which stands for "Only Handle It Once." Basically, this is an acronym for saying that if you start doing something at the beginning of your workday, finish the task before you allow yourself to move onto your next task. If you are constantly switching back and forth between projects, you will have a hard time remembering where you left off and although it seems like you are much more productive, it is actually the opposite because you end up not accomplishing as much as you would if you had just started and worked through the entire task until completion, before moving onto the next one. If you think that following this principle will be too hard for you, we have suggestions. The best way for you to stick to the OHIO principle in your daily routine is to schedule out blocks of time for you to work on your tasks. This includes checking your emails, responding to other messages, checking all of your missed calls and voicemails, and all of the other necessary administrative tasks that might be keeping you distracted during the day. If you do this, instead of stopping everything to respond to an email every time you see one pop up in your inbox, which will undoubtedly incur the extra time to find your place again in the task that you are working on, you only check three times a day. If something is urgent enough, and there is an email that needs to be responded to, don't worry. People should get in the practice of following up an urgent email with a phone call. This would be the best way to get a hold of you and only in the case of real emergencies would you be stopping to address an email rather than doing it every five minutes for requests that may not need to be answered right away. Work on limiting your distractions. When you are working on your projects or tasks that require your ability to focus, you can easily prevent distracting emails, texts, and phone calls and even websites that are likely to tempt you to stop what you are doing and switch from task to task. The best thing you can do for yourself is to turn off your notifications on your desktop and put your phone on silent. If that's not possible, consider putting it in your desk drawer so that it is not in sight and cannot be easily accessed.

Take the Time to Pause

There will always be a little voice inside of our heads that will tell us that we do not have enough hours in the day to take a break. People often tell themselves that they cannot afford the time to slow down as they are only getting paid to keep going at full speed ahead. Believe it or not, the opposite is actually true. The work you are doing is actually too important for you not to slow down and give your mind a break every now and again. Taking breaks helps prevent burn out, and you will be less likely to make mistakes when you give your mind a minute to rest and think about other things for a change. Recent research on this topic has shown that there is a part of the braid that gets really active the moment right before a creative answer to a problem is made aware to us. Neurons that were not previously closely connected now have the opportunity to come together to create new pathways. Taking mental breaks allow the mind to relax and after thinking hard about the same issue that seems to set up the conditions that allow the neurons to regroup and for new ideas to come to us. Taking a walk during your day is a great way to start this type of mental break. Not only can you rest your mind, but you are also getting in some physical exercise that is also good for the rest of your body. This may be useful in our problem-solving tool kit and totally appropriate thing to block out time for. Even if you just take a simple five minutes to sit quietly at your desk with your eyes closed. Short breaks that are similar to this can help refocus your mind, lower your stress levels, and even improve your concentration. Plus, your brain will welcome the break during a hectic work day for everyone. Taking time for yourself during the day is the best thing you can do to manage your time efficiently. Avoiding burn out will keep you focused on your task at hand, and you will be less likely to allow your mind drift and you can get things done at a quicker rate than you thought possible before. Even though it goes against everything, you may think about being more productive, taking breaks are actually very good for improving your time management skills.

Learn How to Say No

You may come to find out that multitasking can make us stupid. From real research done on the topic, it can actually lower our IQ three times as much as smoking cannabis does. Too much input can cause us to experience brain fog. If you want to be successful and see the real results from the projects you are working on, then you should stop taking on more responsibility until you are able to finish one or more of your current projects you are already working on. People will be more understanding if you are continuously saying no and they will be less likely to dump more responsibility on you, thinking that you want to take on more continuously and they do not have to do as much. Saying no will not hurt your career if you are working for the right people. Your managers and supervisors should be more than understanding if you are not taking on as much so that you are producing more quality work on the projects that you already have. The biggest problem we can experience with multitasking is that we are likely going to lower the quality of our work--we are trying to do two things or more at once, and the result is that we do everything less well than if we focused properly on one task at a time. If you are finding that the work you are turning is not as good as it could be, it is likely because you are putting too much on your plate at one time. Limit the amount of work you put on yourself at one time and you will find that you are much more likely to focus more on the task at hand and then you can produce a quality of work that you can be proud of. Although it may seem like it is the right thing to do to say yes to new responsibilities and work constantly, you should learn how to say no when you are at the mental capacity, and you are finding yourself burnt out and not being creative. You will be able to manage your time better if you can say no to projects that do not encourage your best work, and you give yourself the opportunity to finish what you already have going on. Saying no will not hold you back in life; it may actually push you forward because you know what you are capable of and have the time for.

Choose Your Task

There are many times in your workday in which you cannot avoid interruptions, and something urgent will eventually come up. Instead of trying to multitask through these interruptions, you should stop and make yourself a note where you are leaving off in your current project so you can stop that task altogether and focus on the problem that was brought up to you. You can record any thoughts you were having at the moment about your task and how you need to move forward. This gives you the opportunity to deal with the immediate problem before going back to the task you were previously doing. This way, you can accomplish both tasks with the best of your ability, and you will leave yourself with more clues to help you restart the original task more quickly. If you leave it up to yourself to choose your tasks when issues come up, you will feel less stressed about problems coming up as they are likely to do. You can immediately stop yourself and record anything that you were in the middle of thinking about so you do not lose the thought in the event you are on the way to a new idea that could help you finish up the task you are working on.

Ask Yourself Good Questions

When you are in the moments of feeling like you are about to get overwhelmed, you can begin to calm yourself down by asking yourself a series of questions. Begin by asking yourself if this is the best use of your time at the moment. When does this need to be completed? Does this task leverage what I believe my strengths are? Who can I ask for support on this project so that I feel less overwhelmed with the amount of work I have left to do? Coaching yourself to plan your work will be a gift you learn to treasure. You can help yourself work through the work tension you may be feeling and focus your attention on managing your time in a better way so that you are not feeling overwhelmed and you bring your thoughts back to managing your time and working through your projects at a rate that works best for you. Redirecting your thoughts from panic to calm will help you gain control of your emotions so that you do not get burnt out and think that you will never accomplish anything that you have on your plate. Being realistic about your expectations of yourself will let you ask the right questions to bring yourself back to reality.

Give Permission

If you find yourself in the position in which you have realized that you had taken on too much for yourself to handle at the given moment, you can give yourself permission to stop. Recharge yourself and lead by example so that others around you have the same permission to do so in their own lives and their own work. Usually, people do not think that it is okay to slow down or give themselves the permission to, so if you are in a management position, you should take the opportunity to talk to your employees about the power of slowing down and getting more accomplished when you are accepting less work. Find that you are encouraging your employees to focus on the task at hand and turning in quality work rather than taking on more and more to look impressive but never really getting anything done. Give yourself and others the permission to say no; to slow down every now and again so that you can regroup and reset your mind, to where you are not trying to do too much at once. Avoid trying to accomplish two or more things at one time. Even if it takes you a while to do this, you will find that it is very rewarding, and you will be so much better at managing your time that you were previously. This will work in your favor, and you will likely find yourself less stressed with your workload.

These tools are the beginning steps to make sure you are managing your time in a way that will help you be productive during your workday. Banishing multitasking from your workday will also be what you need to focus on your tasks and not jump from thing to thing and not actually getting anything done even though you feel like you are working twice as hard. You may not be able to control all of the emergencies and things that would come up that will break your concentration, but you will be able to handle them much more efficiently without letting it control your entire day and taking more time away from your task than absolutely necessary.

Chapter 5: Learning to Create Amid Chaos

You may be at a point in your life that you see your home life and work life as pure chaos. You may be wondering how you can possibly produce quality work or any work at all when you are continuously working in these types of environments. You will feel like your sense of control is beginning to diminish, and the feeling of being overwhelmed will likely be on the rise. From the noise and distractions of working in an open office to the incoming channels of information, we are constantly monitoring on our cell phones and desktops, quite frankly. It can be difficult for anyone to focus on the things that really matter. Have you ever stopped to think about how distracting your work environment is? Recently, a group of professionals was polled to see what they thought was more distracting: their work environment or their home. More than half agreed that their work environment was much more chaotic than their home. While both of these types of environments are known to be noisy and can be chaotic, at home, these adults had something they felt like they were not able to have at work: the ability to control the chaos around them. This feeling, however, is where a lot of people who feel this way are being mistaken. In reality, we are actually able to control the chaos within our work environments, and we can work to help each other find heightened balance amid workplace chaos. The first step is to feel like you are empowered to take control. If you start to do the work to control the chaos at work, you will find that your hard work will help motivate your coworkers to do the same because they will want the same feelings of control you are experiencing. Before you know it, your workplace will be much calmer, and you and your coworkers will no longer have that overwhelming feeling that the workplace is chaos and they cannot get anything done because of it.

Working at an Optimal Time of the Day

This relates back to our previous chapter in which we suggested you find the time that you are at your peak in your productivity. Find out if you are a morning or evening person when it comes to when you work the best. Know that your biological prime time is when you are at your best to work. If you know that you work best in the morning, try getting into your office or workplace before the rest of your coworkers arrive. If you prefer to work more at night, arrive late, and stay later at the office than the rest of the people in the office. Once you have had the opportunity to figure out your prime working time, you can then take the time to optimize your environment during this time. This will allow you to take your work into a conference room on a floor of your office complex in which no one is there for a few hours during your prime time to get work done, and you can feel more accomplished. Make sure that doing this is approved by your upper management; but if they are working with you to do more for you to enjoy your work environment, they should not have any problems with you altering your environment so that you are comfortable and productive at the same time. If you are a leader or a manager in the workplace, you can also intervene by empowering your employees to choose where they want to work. This means that fewer people who are present in the office at any given time during the day or evening can greatly reduce the amount of chaos you are experiencing in the workplace, especially if your office is an open-concept type setting, which does not allow anyone to be able to hole up in a space that can be quiet and they can be left alone for extended periods of time. Optimizing your workspace will give you the confidence you need in order to be the most productive during the time of day that works the best for you. Figuring it out for yourself in your workplace is the best thing you can do not only for you but for your coworkers as well. You all have the opportunity to work together to make the workplace the best environment for everyone, and this way, you can have many happy workers in an office who are getting a lot more accomplished than they were previously!

Fences Make Great Neighbors

There is a common expression, "weed to seed." The idea behind it is actually pretty simple: we all need to pull the weeds from our emotional and mental gardens for us to watch our seeds grow and flourish. It is pretty easy to begin. You should first start by deciding what it is that you do and not want to do with your life and your job and courageously begin to build a fence to keep out anything that you know will be distracting to you or put you down emotionally. Next, you should then look into the things that you are subscribed to. You should start unsubscribing and continuing to run down the list of things that you can unsubscribe from like news channels, newsletters, or notifications for things that you really do not need or don't have any interest in anymore. Then, you can get to the point where you can start shedding the toxic people in your life. To put it very simply, graciously decline spending time with the people who you do not feel like they excite, inspire, or support you in some way. You do not need any negativity or toxicity in your life, and you do have the power to get rid of it if it is something that does not help you to be a better person. You can also put these into motion into your workplace. This means that if there are things in your workplaces that you would rather not be "subscribed" to, simply remove yourself from the list so that it is no longer a distraction for you. Are there some coworkers that are a constant source of negativity and distraction? Remove yourself from the room or see if you can work in another area of the office so that you are not within a close proximity of them and that you can easily avoid getting swept up in the conversations that can end up lasting all day--not only are you behind on your work, but you are also now leaving work in a foul mood because of the negative talk that you are surrounded by. If you are a leader or a manager in your group, look around and begin to ask yourself if everything and everyone present is contributing to a positive and productive setting. Is there anything or anyone talking over the area and making it negative? Is this dynamic of people and things something you want to continue to cultivate to allow it to grow? Whether you like it or not, sometimes, weeding out toxic personalities in a group of people, especially coworkers, is the best way you can maintain a positive balance in the workplace.

Discover Real and Virtual Filters

Filters can actually be very clarifying, despite what they are usually used for on social media. Using filters in real life will allow us to keep out what we do not want to let into our lives. If you like working by yourself in solitude, you can administer a filter by positioning yourself at work around people who share the same desire to work alone in a quiet environment. In your virtual life, this may mean that you need to find an effective way to mute the noise that distracts you digitally. This means that you may need to start checking your social media accounts only on your phone rather than on your work computer. There are now apps available that keep your social media accounts and apps locked for a certain amount of time to keep you from accessing them during select time periods during the day. It may be a good idea for you to select this option during your core work hours so that you are not being distracted by constant notification of what other people are doing in your virtual world. Because it is on the Internet, it will still be there when you are done working, so you do not feel like you are missing out on something if you do not see it as soon as someone posts it. This will help keep you off your phone and more engaged in the work that is right in front of you. As a leader or a manager of a group of people, there are also some steps you can take to promote filters in your work environment. One step to consider that may be obvious is supporting your employees' desire sometimes to be entirely offline. This means that they are away from their phones and work emails for extended periods of time outside of their typical work schedule. A lot of people are finding themselves constantly staying connected to their work messages, and they do not feel like they are ever able to escape their work life. If you allow your employees to disconnect at night or during the weekends, they will feel a lot better about being able to put those filters up and enjoying life outside of the office. Begin by taking a second look at your policies within the company and the practices you are engaging in on responding to email and messages outside of the working hours.

Paying Attention to Your Mental and Physical Health

The best way to take care of yourself is by taking balanced breaks and rehydrating and avoiding overworking yourself. You will also want to avoid sleep deprivation. Many people state that they are losing sleep over work commitments because they either stay at work until late hours trying to catch up or get ahead, or they are so consumed with emails and work outside of the office that they find it hard to disconnect and fall asleep at night. This also applies to those of us who are the managers or leaders in the group. You need to take care of yourself and your mental and physical health just as much as you take the time to remind your employees to do the same. It is important to use your days off allotted to you, and even though taking vacations can be seen as someone who does not work hard or it may hinder the progression of the workplace for the time being, you should encourage your employees to take time off so that they can come back renewed and in a much better mindset to take on their role than they previously would have been if they were approaching burn out. Employees who see their leaders prioritizing these types of things will feel that it is a good environment to work in and they will also take care of themselves in the same way that you are demonstrating for our own self. If you find yourself as someone who is dreading going to work because the noise levels are out of control or people become too chaotic throughout the day and you are now trying to create the balance you crave, do not assume that only earplugs and patience for your coworkers are going to remedy your situation. Employees, managers, and leaders can all play a role in restoring the balance, so a lot of energy that is always on open spaces appear to have lost along the way. Many open-concept offices are now so loud and without a sense of control that many people are opting out of that type of workplace in favor of those that are more traditional and structured.

Ultimately, although you may think that the only chaotic environment you can control is your home, there are many things and tactics that are available to you so that you can also control your work environment as well. You have the power to make it what you need it to be for you to have the type of workplace where you are at your calmest and most collected so you can focus on your work and limit the number of distractions you come into contact with during your work hours. All of the examples we listed above can be easily brought into the workplace, and if you are an employee, we encourage you to talk to your managers about these things and let them know that you think it would be helpful for a lot of people in the office so that you all can be more productive. If you are the leader or manager, you can look at your employees and see what they would think would be great to incorporate into your environment and that people would find beneficial to their work days. Being flexible as a manager is a positive characteristic to have because you are doing things for your employees to truly enjoy their work and, in turn, they are turning out more quality work because they are thriving in their environments. You can learn how to create work during a choice environment, and you can also learn how to change your environment to make it work better for you so that you can control the crazy and bring it back down to calm. You are not restricted to only controlling your environment at home; it might help you feel more in control of both areas of your life because you can determine what it is that you need to keep your mental health in check. It is also to your benefit to check in on your family members and coworkers as well because they may need your help in figuring out their needs for you to control their own chaos. If people are seeing you being successful in it, they will want to learn from you so that they can have the same calming effect in their lives as well. We encourage you to look at these things that you can implement in your work life and see what works for you.

Chapter 6: Using Social Media Mindfully

Social media has become so ingrained in our lives and daily routines that most people freely admit that scrolling through social media wastes upwards of five hours out of their day every day. iPhone users now have the ability to track how many hours a week they spend on their phones, and they can see if it increases or decreases from week to week. Many people wake up and immediately get on their phones to check their social media accounts for what they had missed while they were sleeping, and they equally check their phones for what they missed throughout the day as they are getting ready for bed at night. Social media has become an all-consuming part of our society, and when you take the opportunity to look up from your own phone and see the world around you, you will find that we are now missing an element of in-person interaction that we all once held very dear to our existence. Social media is now starting to feel more like a burden than a joy to many people who are fully ready to admit that they are addicted to constantly checking their phones and updating their feeds and statuses. There is an information overload when it comes to social media as not only are you getting updates from all of the people you are friends with but now news media outlets are also utilizing social media to get the latest coverage in your hands quicker than traditional outlets can. Social media has become such a time waster for so many people that apps have been developed to where you can eliminate your ability to access certain apps for extended periods of time throughout the day. Many college students use the feature when they are studying so that they do not get distracted with updates from friends and family and spend hours mindlessly scrolling rather than taking the time actually to study. The same thing goes for people who work in an office setting and for those who are freelancers. Many people end up spending more than half their working hours scrolling through social media rather than actually being productive and getting value-added work done. If you are ready to take back your day and do away with time-wasting tasks such as scrolling through social media for hours, you will benefit from reading the simple tips below.

Be Strategic

Many of us are guilty of hopping onto our phones or laptop computers and logging into our social media accounts to get a "quick" recap of the happenings of our friends and family members only to come up for air and realize we have wasted many hours. It is very easy to do, and it is especially easy to do if a hit-or-miss strategy is your sole plan. Now that social media has become so overpowering, you need to get focused on how you are using your time online if you want to be successful in today's world. Being strategic means that you go into each social media scrolling event with a plan of action. This means that you are acting on the purpose of being on social media, and you are stopping yourself short of partaking in time wasting activities. There is nothing wrong with wanting to catch up with friends and family and checking in on someone who just got back forma tropical vacation and with wanting to check out their pictures for inspiration for their next trip. However, there is a time and place to do this. During the workday for multiple hours is not the time or the place to be doing this. If you want to save yourself countless wasted hours on social media, you should start to integrate a plan to which you are keeping yourself away from social media during your prime work hours. If social media is not a large part of your responsibilities, you should eliminate it from your view all together. You should learn how to turn off notification if they are set up on your desktop. You should consider putting your phone notifications on silent and keeping your phone in your desk drawer so that you are not tempted to pick it up every time you see it, or you get a silent notification that your friends are posting or interacting with you on social media. If it is an emergency, people will not contact you over social media, so it is important you keep yourself focused on your work at hand rather than constantly picking up your phone mindlessly for no reason other than to waste time. Keep in mind that managing your social media usage should not be an overwhelming process. Just simply remind yourself what your purpose for using social media is and if it is a good use of your time during work hours or if it is something that can wait until you take a scheduled break to calm your mind down and spend some time catching up with others before you swiftly return back to work.

Engage in Positive Posting

If you are friends with a lot of people on your social media accounts who solely use the platforms for negative talk, and you always feel that you are worse off or in a bad mood once you have spent some time on the apps, it may be in your best interest then to avoid the posts of these people while you are taking a social media break at work. You may find that although you did not get too deep into the posts of your friend, it has a lasting effect on your mood throughout the rest of the day. Many times, even though we do not directly interact with negative people on social media, we are subconsciously affected by their posts, and so we are struggling with positivity and often feel down and out about our own lives and work even though we may not have had any issues that day. If you find that this is happening to you more often than not, you should begin trying to only engage in people who are posting about positive things rather than the negative. Especially on social media apps like Facebook and Instagram, you have the ability to hide the posts of certain people for periods of time without removing them as a friend. You may find this beneficial if you are affected negatively by the things particular people post and if you are finding it is distracting you from your work the remaining parts of the day. Engaging more in positive posting will keep you motivated when you return to work because you are in a good mood and feel about the work that you have ahead of you. Reading encouraging posts will likely have a great effect on you and your ability to stay focused on the remaining work you have that day because you want to better yourself and you work towards being more productive from your social media usage. There are many positive benefits of using social media throughout the day, but as long as you are mindful of what you are viewing and how long you are taking the time to be on it, you should see that you will benefit from it more than you would be negatively affected by it. You will also find that you are not as likely to go down such rabbit holes with positive posts as you would with negative ones because most people do not take the time to comment on positive posts and keep scrolling rather than leaving a trail of drama behind for people to dig into and waste a lot of time engaging with and reading along as other people post.

Experience Now, Share Later

Depending on what type of environment you work in, you may come across different engaging activities during your workday. Social media can quickly become a competition on who is living the best life, and people often go out of their way to engage in activities they might not have others gotten wise into solely so they can post about it on social media. If your office is modern and gives you many different amenities as an employee, you may feel like you want to post about how great it is all the time to keep up with the competition of people who you are friends with. Ultimately, this can lead you to be engaging in one up someone else constantly and you will waste a lot of valuable working time trying to prove that you and your company are better than the rest. Rather than partaking in this kind of behavior during work hours, you should enjoy the experience being given to you by your company and then share it later with friends and family when you are done with work for the day. Now, only does this give you the opportunity to be fully engaged in the activities and truly enjoy yourself, you feel less likely to post something about it because you are engaging in a competition. Being mindful with your social media use means that you are not constantly engaging with posts on social media when you should be taking the time to put your phone down and enjoy what is going on around you. If you find that this is something you do and it is now taking control of your work routine, you may seek out different alternatives to your posting schedule so that you do not feel like it is interrupting your work hours and productivity while you are at work. There is nothing about social media that cannot wait, and you will be much more relaxed at work when you are not constantly fretting over the latest post of your friends and family. You might find that you enjoy your work more when you take the time to sit and focus on that task rather than bouncing back and forth between working and checking social media. If you are afraid that you will miss something or feel like you are not keeping up with social norms by not posting everything as soon as it happens, just know that the Internet is not going anywhere, and what you may have missed while you were working will still be there when you are not.

Block Out Usage Times

If you are not at the point in your social media addiction recovery and you feel like going cold turkey from it, the best thing you can do for yourself is to block out time in your schedule to check it and keep it contained within these set times of consumption. This way, you do not feel like you are constantly being pulled to check your social media accounts, but you are not getting overwhelmed with anxiety for not checking it either. We are not saying that you need to be completely free from social media at work for you to be productive, but being more mindful and strict with your usage can help you stay on track for managing your time and reducing the amount of distraction to expose yourself to during the hours you are working. Slowly but surely, you can continue to limit the amount of time you allow yourself to access your social media accounts until you get yourself to a point where you are content with not looking at social media at all throughout the work day. This can take a lot of work and practice, but being more mindful about your social media usage will not only help you with your productivity and time management but will also help you improve your emotional and emotional health as well. There are many benefits to social media, but not being mindful with it as work can cost you. We hope that these tools we have given you are helpful in getting you to block out more time for your social media usage so that you are not consumed with wasting many hours on social media and not working on your tasks.

Social media has been both a blessing and a curse for many corporations across the world. If you are a leader or manager, and you are struggling with reigning in your employees' social media usage throughout the workday, there are many different avenues you can take to help mediate the amount of time your workers are spending on social media. We do not recommend banning social media use on private networks as it will lead to low morality in the workplace, but working with your employees to come up with ideas can help everyone in the group feel like they are getting the freedom that they would like without the expense of productivity. There are many things that you can do to decrease your own social media usage so that your employees do not feel like you are limiting them but not your own self. Being mindful about your social media usage in the workplace is the best thing you can do for your time management journey as you will find that this may be the number one thing keeping you from being as productive as you would like to be. Always remember that the world is not going to end if you are not checking your social media accounts all the time. The updates will be there when you get a chance to check them, and you will feel more at ease when you are not constantly anxious to check for the latest updates. Help yourself and your health by being mindful about your social media usage, and you will find that you can bring this over into your own social life as well. You will benefit from not having to work late hours for making up the time you were not productive when you have had deadlines approaching. There is nothing worse than having to explain why your part of a task is late because you spent too much time being on your phone and not actually working on the task at hand. Don't be that guy! People will find you are much more trustworthy when you take on a task and finish it in an appropriate amount of time because you are not being lazy and getting distracted by social media.

Chapter 7: Reconsider Being Constantly Connected

Research shows that people are increasingly seeking to be on a 24/7 digital connection while they are driving, in their bedrooms, and in their social and family lives. There are not many people who don't sleep next to their phones and take devices on first dates and are digitally connected while eating every meal. These people strive to be "always on." When you are this open and available, however, it is harder to choose to ignore your work emails and messages that can come through from your office at all hours of the day, even on weekends. You may even be hearing from your boss late on a Saturday night when they know you will always be readily available to take their call. Many companies require that their employees be available 24/7, and most employees don't actually have a problem with it because their phones are already in the hand as it is. People see it as an advancement opportunity always to be working and being available for their bosses and clients, which means that they are the best person for the job and for the upcoming promotion. It has gotten so much harder for individuals to know how to shut down and quit working when they know that all they are doing is taking a short break on their commute home just to open their computer's back up or to constantly be replying to emails on their phone after they have already returned home for the evening instead of spending time with their friends and family. In the old days, there used to be such a thing that people referred to as work-life balance, but these days, the lines get more and more blurred as we are constantly digitally connected and technology makes it easier to always be in constant contact with one another. Not answering emails and phone calls on the weekend have now become the odd behavior as it has slowly become commonplace that people bring their work home and spend time catching up on work tasks on the weekends. We are seeing more and more issues with people experiencing burn out at the jobs and millennials are being spoken about as a generation who cannot stay at a job longer than a year. But in reality, the expectations of them to constantly be performing have become draining, and they are seeking an alternative job that may give them more sense of control of their lives and how they spend their time.

The concept of work-life balance largely came before the digital technology age. The term came about roughly 100 years ago, but back then, people were actually taking physical papers home to finish up their work for the day. Now that we can be constantly connected and have the ability to round-the-clock digital response and connection, the lines are officially blurred between work and home. Research shows however, that more and more millennials are wanting their home life to be just that: 100% home life without the interruption of work responsibilities. A global study that was conducted shows that millennials and millennial parents are very serious about finding a work life balance so much that they are willing to relocate if that means they can move into a job that offers it. Employees want the ability to bring their own personal devices into work to check their social media whenever they want, and they also want to shut the door on their work responsibilities when they get home. Millennials were surveyed and were shown to be more willing than other generations to pass up promotions, change jobs, and take a pay cut to achieve a flexible schedule. As much as people want to be able to check their devices at work but not do the same for their work at home often find that it is harder to resist in the digital age. Technology is the enabler of poor work-life balance, and precedents to bring your work home have been quickly established in this technology age. Oftentimes, this is because people are spending so much time on their personal devices during work hours that they have no choice but to bring work home because of the lack of progress they made while they were at the office. Then, you enter into a perpetual cycle of working at home and constantly being connected because you find yourself not ever being able to get ahead because of the number of digital distractions you are facing at work. Being constantly connected is becoming a downfall for this particular generation because the only connections they are making are digital. Most people can go an entire work day without any face-to-face interaction with their coworkers and often rely on email and instant messaging services to get the information they need from one another rather than take a few steps to the cube over and having a face-to-face conversation about it.

It is clear from the research that has been conducted that many people are finding themselves pressured always to be available. Most are definitely not happy about it. As the generations that are used to being digitally connected continue to come up through the workforce, the notion of constantly being accessible to everyone and everything will continue to be the corporate office norm. As the shift to this type of work culture continues, the implications of a never-ending workday can change the ways that our current companies are doing business and they will have the potential to radically change what it means to be an employee in the digital age. Companies who are jumping on the constantly connected bandwagon will begin to find themselves in a dilemma of which they can enable their employees to communicate with ease and still strive to protect their privacy and personal time outside of the office. Companies will continue to embrace the change so long as their employees continue to show and prove that they are willing to be constantly connected. It is on the employees to push back against this era if they are at the point where they feel like they have a lack of sense of control in how often they can shut off their workday and enjoy quiet. If you find that your work is taking over all areas of your life, and you are talking about work and doing work more than you can enjoy time with friends and family doing things that you love to do, it may be time for you to take a step back out of this digital age and reconsider being constantly connected. Social media breaks are becoming increasingly popular as people are finding that being constantly connected virtually is taking a toll on their mental health. The same can be true for real-life work and being constantly available to answer questions and to work on projects at the moment. Everyone should be able to enjoy downtime without having to be glued to their phones to answer an email as soon as it hits the mailbox or answer every phone call when someone has an issue or has a question. We, as a society, should go back to the era where we actually take the vacation days we are allotted and simply disconnect from the digital world for a few days to reconnect with the physical world around us.

Being constantly connected to the office has proven to decrease productivity. From what we had discussed above, human typically needs a break in order to continue to thrive. Having your mind constantly connected to a task or a problem at work will eventually wear someone out. They will no longer be performing at the peak expected of them simply because they are burnt out and tired. You may have found yourself in a similar situation where you have tried to work for too long without taking a break to change your mindset briefly and you have seen your productivity decline. The number of hours varies from person to person, but studies have shown that working more hours actually decreases a person's productivity output per additional hour worked. Many of us know when we are tired and stressed out from working too much--this is often when we start making dumb mistakes. It is also possible for us to make poor decisions and exercise poor judgment when it comes to solving problems or looking for solutions. Humans simply cannot continue to put out their top quality work when they are struggling to stay mentally focused and pay attention to the task at hand. Constantly working ultimately causes more problems that it will solve for a company. Not only will consumers not be getting the best quality, but it also makes employees enjoy what they are doing for work less and less as time goes on. Resentful employees usually do not last long and, in turn, you will find many people are leaving their positions in search of more balance between their work and their personal life. People nowadays are less likely to stick with a job that they hate, and one that has them constantly working will quickly become one that they hate. A good boss and good corporation or company must understand that in order to retain the best employees and keep the moral in the position upward, the employees must have downtime to recharge and relax so that they can come back to the workforce and continue to do and want to do the best job that they can. If you find that you constantly have to do rework or you are missing deadlines simply because you are too tired to perform at your highest level for extended periods of time, you should consider unplugging for an extended period of time to see if this will help you regain some of your energy levels and motivation to be doing your best work each and every day. It does not come off as failure or weakness to give yourself the opportunity to take a break or a vacation to recharge and reset your mind to be more open to accepting new tasks.

This may be an obvious fact to state, but research has shown that employees who are constantly connected for an extended period of time are reported to give more stress than their coworkers who take the time to disconnect. If you have a boss or are a boss who is connected 24/7, it is likely contributing to the stressful environment people are experiencing when they work in a constantly connected workplace. If you are a boss who is striving to be connected at all times, you will likely find yourself continuously stressed out, and eventually, you will start taking it out on your employees which creates stress for them as well. A boss that is consistently hovering or always asking questions or shooting off texts and emails at all hours of the day will only serve as a compound for employees who are already stressed about their own work level and stressors at home. If everyone in the work force is feeling stressed out, it might be a good opportunity to take the time to give employees mid-day breaks and offer incentives to take breaks so that the stress levels in the office do not get to the point that they are overwhelming. The last thing a good company or manager should want to go is to work their employees to death and ultimately decrease the morale among employees and lead them to get sick or having issues with mental health. It is a benefit to the company to give their employees time to disconnect once they leave the office so that they can return to work the next day fresh and ready to tackle issues that they may not have had the mental capacity for previously. It is a benefit to everyone to consider reducing the number of hours you are digitally connected throughout the day. If something is of a serious matter, there are ways to get a hold of people to fix the problem in a timely manner, but usually, something that we are connected for can usually wait in till the next work day. People find that they are being contacted for simple issues that are not detrimental to the operations of the workplace, and they strive to cut out all of the unnecessary engagement outside of regular business hours. Being mindful of other's time and responsibilities outside of work hours will help everyone reach a point where they can feel comfortable taking time out to recharge and push work tasks aside for a few hours.

Ultimately, we should all consider taking a step back from our work responsibilities and consider unplugging every now and again. Not only would it have extreme benefits on your mental health, but it will also help you to retain your levels of productivity and creativity as an employee. You should never let yourself get to the point where your job is having a negative effect on your health. Employers are becoming much more understanding of the effects that being constantly connected can have, and there are many companies that are striving to give their people a better work-life balance. Reconsider being constantly connected if you find yourself in a similar situation as we described above and you will likely find that you are in a better position to manage your time according to what you need to get through your day. Taking breaks is the best thing you can do for yourself and your creativity, and employers should respect your need to be away from work for periods of time so you can enjoy time with family and friends. Sometimes, your best ideas will come from being completely disconnected from the problem and thinking about totally unrelated topics. Stepping back in a way in which you are giving yourself the opportunity to explore different avenues of things that you are interested in will allow you to apply that creativity you are striving for in areas outside of that activity. Most people find that when they give themselves the opportunity to partake in a creative endeavor, they are able to come up with much better solutions to workplace problems than they would have if they sat consistently thinking about the problem and stressing over how to find the right solution.

Chapter 8: Reclaim Self-Respect

People dedicate their time to what they value the most. If you do not have the self-respect you need to value yourself and your time, your time will not be valued by any standard, and it will eventually end up being wasted by who and what you allow to waste it. The definition of self-worth comes as a noun; it means the sense of one's own value or worth as a person. This term can be used hand in hand with the idea of self-respect. The definition of time management is the ability to plan and control how you spend the hours in your day to effectively accomplish your goals. How do these two things relate? Here's the connection. If you do not have a sense of who you are as a person and respect that version of yourself and have the ability to adapt your values based on who you are around, you end up like a kite in the wind being tossed around and eventually you are likely to find that people are taking advantage of you because you are an easy target. Many times, when we do not have enough self-respect, we allow people to treat up poorly and take advantage of us because we are not accepting of the fact that we deserve better. We often think that the way people treat us is how we deserve to be treated, when in reality, if we had the self-esteem and respect to stand up for ourselves others would be more likely to have the same level of respect for us. This is usually why people stay in toxic work environments because people believe that it will be like that anywhere they go and that they do not have enough self-respect to stand up for themselves when their bosses expect them to work a lot of overtime to make up for the slack of others who are not doing the same. If you have the opportunity to reclaim yourself respect in the work environment, you will find that you are going to set yourself up to be in a great position to get the things you want out of your career while also being able to effectively manage your time better because you are not getting others workload put onto you because you cannot stand up for yourself and say no when more and more is being asked of you.

When you do not honor your own time, you should not be surprised when others do not as well. Most people will define you and respect you based on how you do these things for yourself. You should be valuing yourself within your job and company to which you can set boundaries on what is conformable for you and stay true to those boundaries so that you are not getting overworked and burnt out. Most boundaries are created when people violated a value of someone's, and they are looking to take control back of their own lives. Boundaries are healthy ways of expressing your values to others without making them feel like you are not willing to see their side of things as well. You do not need to go with the crowd if they are doing something that is not a value of yours or goes against a boundary you have set. You should have the self-respect to say no and move on from the group even if they are judging you or make fun of you. In the workplace, you should also be able to learn how to respectfully and professionally say no to people who are pushing your boundaries. If your boss is expecting you to work 7 days a week, you have the right to say no because you have set boundaries to allow yourself personal time outside of the office. If you have self-respect and push for what you believe in, others will see that and they will respect your decision. If you falter on your values and allow others to tell you how you feel and what you should do all the time, you will not get the respect you deserve and you will often start doing things that go against your values. Often in your work environment, you can be bullied into doing things that you do not want to do based on peer pressure or pressure from the higher-ups in the company. Many people feel like they have to do everything they are told for them to remain in good standing with the company, but this is not always the case. Just know that when you do set boundaries and are trying to stick to them, your boundaries will likely be tested more often than you think. People whom you surround yourself with, if they do not share the same boundaries as you, are the ones who are likely to test them. It is good to surround yourself with people who share similar values and boundaries as you so that you can work comfortably in your space knowing you will not need to be conscious of the people you work with. Likely, you will have coworkers who have different values and boundaries as you, but it is important you stand your ground while also respecting the other person's boundaries as well. You need to put out into the world what you want to receive. You cannot expect your boundaries to be respected if you are not doing the same for other people.

People are likely not respecting your time and boundaries because they are trying to satisfy their own priorities. You might find your coworkers are making increasing demands on your time at work and during non-work hours as well. Hundreds of emails are threading your inbox as well as messages and whatever else type of communication your office uses. Your day is already full, and it can sometimes be a bit much to handle. The only reason people are taking your time and running away with it is that you are allowing them to do it. They do this because it helps them accomplish their own priorities, but how does the correlate with your own priorities? Keep in mind that no one will really care about your priorities except for yourself. This why if you are finding people are not respecting your time, you need to reclaim it for yourself. This is the best way for you to garner yourself respect and allow yourself to manage your time better, so you are not overworked and feeling anxious about getting your own work done. If you are not communicating your values and work load to others, they are not going to respect your time because they truly do not know what your workload is and how much you have going on in your own world. We are not saying you need to share every detail with others about your personal life, but it is important you communicate your values and your workload so that others will know to respect your time and not push more onto you that you likely would not be able to handle. Oftentimes, leaders in your group may have an "ignorance is bliss" attitude. If they do not know what you are working on and how much you have going on already, leaders will feel free to pie more tasks onto you throughout the day. If you do not push back and say that you cannot accomplish all of your usual tasks, plus the new additional on that day, then it is on you, not your leader. It is your responsibility to manage your own workload and let people know when you have hit your boundary of work you can take on for that day. It may take some practice, but you will feel much better about the situation in your workplace. When you start respecting yourself, and others start respecting you, people are more likely to come for you for help in different ways rather than just fishing work off onto you.

You can build yourself respect and take back your time without having to announce it to everyone around. People will likely get upset with you because you are trying to reclaim your time. It is understandable that you cannot be expected to turn your phone off whenever you want because you simply cannot go long periods of time without being contactable for long periods of time, especially if you are in a position where people need to get in touch with you easily. You may not be able to cut off communication all together, but there are ways in which you can concentrate on removing the most invasive and distracting forms of communication you come in contact with everyday and usually multiple times a day. You do have the ability to work in offline mode in your email if you find that your email notifications are becoming too distracting for you to get your work accomplished. This is an important first step in understanding which communication methods you use are the most distracting to you in your day. Usually, for most people, it is definitely email. If someone calls you, it is usually because they need to get with you on something right away; therefore, it has an embedded sense of emergency that comes with it. With your email, however, it is up to your discretion to figure out if a message is urgent or not. Messages coming through can range from details on your upcoming office Christmas party to reminding everyone to clean out the fridge for the weekend or a message from a stakeholder whom you do not have time to think about right now. Emails are often unrelated to the task you are currently working on right now. A simple solution to avoiding disruptive email distractions is to work in offline mode for 30 to 60 minutes at a time. Since email is not engaging in real time as a phone call would be, you have the ability to hold off on responding right away for the meantime until you give yourself a break from the task and you can spend a few moments responding to emails. If someone sends you an email and follows it up with a phone call, then you know that it is something that needs your attention right away and is probably urgent. Putting your email into an offline mode to focus on your priorities at the given moment will help you manage your time and get more accomplished. You will be amazed at how much our productivity will go up once you put this into practice.

Give yourself the opportunity to get away from your desk. It is amazing how easy it is to withdraw from the workplace from time to time and how good of a positive effect it will have on your body. You know how sometimes when you call in sick, and everyone leaves you alone for the day knowing that you won't be in the office and likely not available to help? The world will still go on without you, and things will get prioritized differently so that they will still get done regardless. We are not saying to call in sick when you are not actually sick. Sometimes, booking yourself a meeting room to work privately for an hour away from your desk helps you get so much done. People will not be able to find you at your desk so they often just wait until they see you again instead. When you eventually return to your desk and people ask where you were, you can honestly say that you were around, but you were in a meeting or working elsewhere. You won't be lying to your coworker because you were technically in a meeting with yourself, and it was likely the most productive meeting you had in a while! Many times, conference rooms are not available to claim for hours of just personal alone work, so if your office gives you the ability to travel with your computer, you should also use your other resources to get away from your desk but still get work done. Most offices have common areas where you can sit and eat while not at your desk. If you know that there are times of day when no one is using these common spaces, you can use that to your advantage in that way so you can get alone time to work in a different environment, but you are not hogging valuable meeting space if that's not why you are actually using it. Giving yourself a few valuable hours of time by yourself a day will help minimize your distractions from others and gives you a sense of self-respect because you are regaining control of your time to get stuff done without coworkers distracting you with their own task problems or simply just wanting to talk to catch up. You can be creative in ways to get time to yourself without removing yourself from your work environment entirely.

These are some simple things you can do in your office environment that will allow you to take back your self-respect in the office and better manage your time and workload. It is important that you respect yourself and your time so that others will do the same. If you find certain managers and coworkers particularly difficult, it does not hurt to have a professional conversation with them so that you are not adding to your stress level on top of an already demanding schedule. It is up to you to decide how much you can handle, and taking on more work when you simply do not have the time will lessen your productivity and will likely not get you any respect in the office because people will not only dump their own responsibilities on you, but they will not respect your time and think that you can't handle your tasks. Keep working towards your goals of managing your time so that you can feel yourself become more confident in your abilities to get all of your work done for you to enjoy time outside of the office and not have to constantly be thinking about your work or tasks you have not yet completed. Self-respect is not just a good thing to have in the office but also in your personal life as you will likely find yourself faced with similar scenarios in your life outside of the office as well.

Chapter 9: Letting Go of Perfectionism

Being too good at something can really mess up your ability to manage your time. If you are prone to perfectionism, which is classified as a good characteristic, and you do not do something to control it or keep it reigned into where it does not start to affect your daily life and habits, there will likely be tragic consequences up ahead in the very near future. People classified as perfectionists tend to only think about the first part of the definition of what perfectionism is. The first half of the definition is "a good characteristic." For them, many people who are perfectionist are the title like a badge of honor. Perfectionists are often known to be overachievers, demanding flawlessness in everything, their appearance, their relationships, and most commonly, the work they produce. If you are not someone who is doing work for the government or working with nuclear weapons, you may want to do yourself a favor and ease up on the perfectionism to help not only your stress levels but your ability to achieve time management as well. People who are perfectionists often work long hours well into the night because they try to correct and fix every little thing about a project or task before turning it in. Oftentimes, their work is already at top levels, but they are so concerned with being perfect that they analyze every little detail and find problems that may or may not actually exist. Perfectionists do everything with 100% and then some, but often they are known to be exhausted and overworked because they put so much pressure on themselves to be flawless. It is commonly very hard to have relationships with people who are true perfectionists because they will pick apart everything about the relationship as well as the person they are in a relationship with to maintain a perfectly complete image to the outside world. Perfectionists work tirelessly until they complete a project they could absolutely find no flaws in, even if it means working all day and night and turning the project in at the last minute before it is due. On the surface, especially to employers, this sounds like a really amazing trait to find in someone who is going to be on your team. Finding someone who will stop at nothing to do everything right and produce perfect work every single time? What a dream! Certainly, perfectionism has its benefits. It is a great motivator for people who are searching for achieving great results. Attention to detail and thorough research and a level of intense focus often lead to the highest quality outcomes, and perfectionists have all of these characteristics within them.

Psychologists describe perfectionists as people who often get hung up on meaningless details and spend more time on projects than necessary. The result of being in a single-minded focus such as perfectionism is ultimately a reduction in productivity. Do you find yourself as someone who spends too much time weighing your options? A negative outcome that also comes along with being a perfectionist type is procrastination. If a perfectionist is working on a project that has few defined parameters and hard end date, a perfectionist can find themselves in analysis paralysis, which is that no man's land where over complicating a situation can lead to a black hole of indecision. Perfectionists often spend so much time going back and forth between the options they have to make a decision that it is really unlikely that they make a decision in a timely manner. Being a person who wants to do their best every day and every time they are submitting something is an admirable quality to a point, and there are some situations where cutting corners is simply not an option. However, if you are waiting for your time and resources by attempting to achieve perfection in your day-to-day tasks, you are ultimately wasting a lot of time. You are also likely hindering your productivity and possibly creating a bottleneck for your team. Most likely, you are doing both in your everyday life. This means that the heart of your issues is a time management problem. While having high standards of yourself is paramount to being successful in your career, having unrealistic expectations of yourself as well as your coworkers can negatively impact your relationships, your self-esteem, and your career. Perfectionism is not always a bad thing, but there are many negative connotations to perfectionism if you do not learn how to control it and end up letting it control you.

Perfectionism can stem from work and encroach into your everyday life, and you will find that you are stressing yourself out unnecessarily because you are always trying to be perfect in everything you do and say. The perfectionism you will find is often a huge time waster because you spend so much time in the initial stages of a project thinking through all of your options, and once you finally are getting to work on the project, you are already very far behind. Then, you will have to fight through taken so much time to finish it because you want the final result to be perfect. Working through your issues with perfectionism can really help manage your time better as you will be spending less of it on time wasting activities associated with perfectionism.

Are you a perfectionist? Based on the information we have provided in this chapter so far, and by answering the following questions, you should get a better idea on if you can qualify yourself as a perfectionist. Does every project, regardless of its size, get treated with the same amount of urgency and get equal attention? Are you frequently coughed in analysis paralysis using much of your time on the project weighing your options before you take any action on completing the project? Do you often feel frustrated that you do not have enough time to finish a project? If you answered yes to all or some of these questions, you might have varying levels of perfectionism. There are other tell-tale signs of perfectionism that you should consider. Perfectionists focus on the outcome, not on the journey. They are noticing the small imperfections in their work and others rather than the overall result of the project. Perfectionists do not want to participate in something that they do not excel at. And finally, perfectionists have difficulty delegating tasks to others for fear that they might not get the task done correctly. If you see these traits in yourself, you have a tendency to lean towards perfectionism. There are ways to balance your need for perfection within your limitations in terms of your time and available resources. Knowing and understanding that you are a perfectionist is the first time in trying to control your perfect tendencies and getting back to being able to manage your time effectively. There are some simple things that you can start to do and include in your day-to-day life so that you can finally find calm in your routine and know that you are staying on the task rather than letting your mind veer off into the unknown of not being able to make a decision and move your project forward. If you are already aware that you are a perfectionist and you are looking for ways to control the symptoms of being a perfectionist so that you can manage your time better, we have the following tips for managing your time as a perfectionist. Because perfectionists are often hindered by self-doubt or exceptionally high standards, they often miss deadlines. The following tips can help you keep your work on track and keeping your organization goals in your focus for your future goals:

1. Despite whatever your instincts are likely telling you to do, assign an urgency and priority level to each task that you need to accomplish. All tasks that you have to do are not equal in their priority or urgency. It is in your DNA to put forth your best effort for everyone one of your projects, but not all projects need the exact same level of intensity. Working through figuring out what is a priority and what is not is something that will take practice, but it is the first step in trying to figure out how to control your perfectionism.

2. Think about getting a second opinion. If you are not sure how you should prioritize your projects, it might be a good idea to talk to your team leader or coworker to see if they have ideas on how you can manage your task list in a better way. Everything may feel to you like it is a high-value project. There could actually be some items on your list so that they can be identified, while the other items can be moved further down your to-do list so you can focus on what should be prioritized first and the fewer ones after those are completed.

3. Get to work. As we discussed earlier, a close cousin to perfectionism is procrastination. If you feel like you cannot begin a project until you have already reached the perfect solution to a problem you may face, you

should just go ahead and dive into the project anyway. It is admirable that you want to get everything right the first time around but not when it is done at the expense of deadlines and customer commitments. If you are doing this often enough, it can damage your reputation, and it could ultimately hurt your job security. Even if you do not have all of the details to start a project in a way that you might feel most comfortable, start wherever you can start while you wait for the rest of the information to find its way to you eventually.

4. Set limits for yourself. If you have a tendency to work and do a lot of reworks on a task way past its deadline, set a time limit for yourself. Physical timers can be effective tools to help you manage your time to spend on a particular task. When the timer goes off, move on to the next thing you need to work on. When the final deadline for the project approaches, hand your work off to another person to get a quick run through to get another perspective on the quality of the work performed rather than solely relying on yourself knowing that you will likely pick apart every minimal detail and end up turning the project in late.

5. Be realistic. You need to realize that not everything can be perfect and know that not everything is expected to be perfect. Do not give up on your work, though. No one

likes to make mistakes, but just because you make mistakes when you turn something in and may have to redo it doesn't mean that your initial work is not worth doing. Knowing that your work is the best you can perform at that moment in the amount of time that you allotted will help manage your stress when you are working through all of your tasks.

6. Cut some slack for other people. Watch out for the overly critical attitude you may have towards those who you work with. Not only can it alienate your colleagues from wanting to work with you on projects but it can also hurt your chances of having the opportunity to promote or advance up in the company when you are seen as a person who can be difficult to work with. When you are less critical of yourself, you can be less critical of others; therefore, you can have good relationships with others when you are working together through projects. If you are known around the office as someone who is easy to work with and is a good collaborator, people will often be more willing to help you out when you are in situations where you need a second opinion or someone to wrap up a project for you since you may not have the time to do it yourself.

7. Keep the big picture in mind. If you are having trouble wrapping up the end of a project because it is not quite at the level that you expect it to be perfect, ask yourself this: how will the additional work affect the outcome of the project? Will the end results really be vastly improved? Will you be turning the project in late? If your perfectionism is really hurting you rather than helping you and the project you are working on, it is probably best that you adjust your behavior. If you are really struggling with figuring out how to end a project reach out to others for help. They may have ideas on how to wrap something up so you can do a quick check before you hand it in. You should never turn in something late because you are nitpicking the finer details on it and things that do not really matter for the big picture and the actual project that you turn in.

Bottom line: there is nothing wrong with wanting to do a good job in your career and the projects you work on. The key is knowing when good is good enough and acceptable to turn in to your managers. You must learn how to balance your own expectations of your work with the expectations of your leadership and management teams. You should save perfection for the projects where it is going to be seen and valued by all of those involved. Projects of lesser value do not need to be perfect because it is likely to get overlooked, and you may become discouraged if no one else takes the time to value the work that you have created. Identifying your perfectionism tendencies that are known to hamper your output is the first real step in understanding how they impact your work life as well as your personal relationships. Being more self-aware and open to adjusting your thought processes makes it much easier for you to improve your time management skills and ultimately improving your levels of productivity as well.

Chapter 10: A Call to Action

We have spent the entirety of this book giving you opportunities to identify how you can better improve your time management skills. You are probably wondering what the true benefits of time management are. There are so many benefits to working on how you manage your time. Overall, not only will it help you be more productive at work and home, but you will also find that you can enjoy your life outside of work more than you would have been able to before. People who feel that they are good time managers often say that, since they got a handle on managing their time, they have felt less stressed and more in control of their schedules in a way they had not been able to experience before. If done right, time management can be a huge benefit in your life. Not only will it give you the opportunity to accomplish more in your life but it can also help you in relation to others, your health, and so many more things positively. Being less stressed because you are accomplishing more helps not only your physical health but also your mental health. You are more likely to engage in activities where you can be happy because you now feel like you have time to do those things when you likely didn't feel that way before. This chapter is your call to action to finally take control of your life and figure out how to begin managing your time. There is nothing but benefits that come from it, and we look forward to finding that this book has been a huge help for you to accomplish your goals and working toward being the best employee you can be without reaching toward perfectionism.

Below are the top benefits of finding your ability to manage your time. This should be motivating enough for you to start the process of being a better manager of your time.

1. Accomplish More

    First of all, one of the biggest benefits of time management is that you will now have the ability to accomplish more than you ever thought possible. When you take the time to prioritize your tasks and compartmentalize your problems and work towards solutions in effective ways, you will find that you are getting more things done that you would have previously. This, however, does not necessarily mean that you are just getting more done. You may actually be finding that you are crossing off fewer tasks on your to-do list once you are managing your time efficiently. What accomplishing more with time management means is that you are getting more of the important things done, and when you do what is high on the priority list, you are accomplishing far more than simply finishing a to-do list of things that probably could have waited until you finished up the high priority tasks.

2. Feel Accomplished

Now that you are accomplishing a lot more, you will also be feeling accomplished. This, in turn, makes you feel better about yourself. Many of us have had days where we are stuck in the weeds all day long. We are working so hard and at the end of the day feel like we never actually got one thing accomplished. Effective time management helps solve this problem. Feeling accomplished helps you reach out to other things that might interest you, and you will leave work feeling good rather than dreading going back to the office in the morning. This also helps you not have to bring work home at the end of the day so you can spend quality time with your family and friends instead of working until all hours of the night and not having a social life.

3. Less Stress

Another great benefit of time management is that you will feel like you are a lot less stressed. You will be less stressed in both your career as well as your home life. When you are very busy doing all of your urgent tasks that come along, and you feel like you are not able to accomplish all of the things that you need to get done in a day, or you simply feel overwhelmed by all of the responsibilities you have, it can create a lot of stress. Being stressed for extended periods of time can hurt your productivity, your relationships with your boss, coworkers, employees and it will eventually hurt both your physical and mental health as well. If you get good at managing your time, it will help reduce the amount of stress you feel.

4. Less Overwhelm

Have you ever found yourself in a situation where you're so overwhelmed that there was nothing you could do except sit there and do nothing at all? Many people who do not know how to manage their time find themselves in this situation more often than not. The truth behind being a working adult, however, is that you will really never have enough time to do everything you want to do. You definitely do not need to do everything either. Effective time management will help you focus on what is the most important to get rid of what is not and help you feel less overwhelmed and less stressed, so you feel at ease with your life and responsibilities.

5. Less Rushed

Being able to manage your time will also help you feel less rushed. When you are approaching a deadline for a project, and you have managed your time successfully instead of rushing through the days to get it completed, you will find yourself at a point where you are already where you need to be to turn the projection on time. If you always feel stressed and overwhelmed and focused on urgent things, you are always going to feel rushed to the finish. When you can manage your time well, it will help you rather focus on the important. Fight the urge to focus on the urgent and to let you work without feeling so rushed all of the time.

6. Fewer Problems

Effective time management will also reduce the number of problems that you face when working through a project which, in turn, reduces your overwhelm and stress, and it will ultimately help you get more done. If you are less focused on being overwhelmed, you can focus on the task at hand and put forth your best work the first time around rather than having to redo things multiple times because you are so focused elsewhere that you miss things that you should be fixing before you turn something in. Have you ever forgotten an appointment or something that you promised that you would do by a certain time? Managing your time efficiently will help you minimize the tendency to forget things done.

7. Less Rework

Rushing through a project, elevated levels of stress, and being overwhelmed with a task at hand can cause more mistakes and details to be forgotten. When you can manage your time well, you will spend less time having to redo projects and tasks which then bring more stress and overwhelm into the equation. Less rework also helps you feel confident in the work you are turning in because you do not have to worry about the quality of work you are putting out because you have given yourself the amount of time needed to complete the task in a way which is good quality and no rework would be needed.

8. Stand Out

Being known as someone who is good at managing their time well will help you stand out among your other coworkers and likely your friends in your personal life as well. Many people are wasting their time at their jobs and are very inefficient at their work and how they are going about their days are extremely ineffective. When you manage your time well, you will accomplish a lot more, and it makes you look good towards your bosses. Plus, you are more likely to be looked at for future projects and better promotional offers. Many companies will likely hire you knowing that you do not need to be micromanaged to get your work done.

9. Get Promoted Faster

When you are accomplishing more, and you are known for being someone in the office who is really good at managing their time well, you are much more likely to get promoted faster and move up the ladder to management in your company. Not only that, if you find yourself looking for a new job, you have to be effective in what you are accomplishing. You are likely to get hired faster with having a proven track record of success. You are setting yourself up for great future potentials, and managing your time is the best way to get there in the least invasive way as possible.

10. Earn More Money

With getting promoted faster and managing your time better, you will be on the route to earning more money at a faster rate than others. When you are doing your job effectively, your company will be much more likely to pay you what you are worth, and they will be happy to compensate you for a job well done. You will have a lot more room to negotiate in your performance reviews because you will have a proven past of being the best and knowing what to do to manage your time and taking on new responsibilities at the same time.

11. Less Effort

Effective time management can also help you accomplish more without having to put forth as much effort to do so. People look to being good at time management as a burden rather than a tool for success. There is a famous quote that says every minute spent planning saves 10 minutes in execution. Many people who are not good at time management will waste time trying to remember what tasks they have to do and eventually working on things that are not the important ones or things that they can wait to work on after the important ones are finished. They will never take the time to improve their skills and will waste so much time trying to research things or items and figure out what they need to do. It is a vicious cycle many people fall into, and reducing this from your daily routine will be a lifesaver. You should be working smarter and not harder, and time management is the first step in being able to do this.

12. Focus More on Your Priorities

If you are trying to make more time for your family and friends outside of work, you need to prioritize them over finishing up a project. If you manage your time effectively, you can finish up tasks on time and find yourself going home from work at a decent hour. In turn, you can spend more time with your family and friends and focus on important things outside of your career. Many people waste so much time at work and then work extra hours and bring their work home. While we sometimes have our priorities wrong, for many, if they manage their time more efficiently, the need to bring your work home will become less and less, and you will not feel the pressure and stress to be on call constantly.

13. Manage Interruptions

One of the biggest work distractions that we all face in our day-to-day at the office is distractions from other people. Whether they are talking about non-work related things or are constantly sending email and texts about things that are not urgent or even important, we can find ourselves getting sucked up into an endless spiral of not getting anything done because we are constantly distracted by the constant communication we are in contact with. These distractions from other people can be legit cries for help or more often a waste of time. We discussed in previous chapters how to get yourself away from the interruptions for you to have your time managed better. Either way, when you learn how to manage your time effectively, you can learn how to deal with interruptions professionally and you can be proactive in managing your day appropriately.

These are just some of the many things that you can feel good about when you learn how to be someone who is good at time management. You have many things to look forward to as you are going through the process of being a good time manager and, although it is a lot of work, the end results are definitely worth the work. Time management skills are absolutely the best thing you can do for yourself if you are looking to make a positive change in your life.

Conclusion

Congratulations and thank you for making it all the way to the end of *Time Management*. Let's hope it was informative and able to provide you with all of the tools you need to achieve your goals whatever they may be

We hope that you find yourself in a better position than you were when you started. We have worked hard to provide you with the best knowledge to help on your journey through time management and how easy it will be for you to become a pro in it, in no time. Feel free to refer back to certain parts of this book if you find yourself stuck in your journey of getting better at managing your time. It always helps to push through a plateau when you look back and pick up something you may have missed in the first go around of reading the book.

Time Management is a one-stop shop to learning how to be your best self and work towards being able to get more done at work, in order to spend more time at home with your friends and family. You will find that you are in a good position to be the employee you want to be, and simple things you can add to your routine is all you need to do to get where you want to be. Being skillful in time management is a great characteristic to have; it is highly sought after in many organizations and life relationships as well. No one wants to date or be married to someone who cannot seem to manage their time efficiently every day.

www.ingramcontent.com/pod-product-compliance
Lightning Source LLC
Chambersburg PA
CBHW070807220526
45466CB00002B/587